Mental Warfare

By

Breuna Walker

GW01057583

Preface

Welcome to *Mental Warfare*, a journey through the complicated and turbulent landscape of mental health. This collection of poems dives into the inner battles that many of us face, exploring the raw and unfiltered emotions associated with mental health conditions such as anxiety, depression, OCD, PTSD, and more.

The title, *Mental Warfare*, details the ongoing battle within the mind – a struggle that can feel isolating and relentless. Yet, this collection is not solely about struggle. It also highlights the resilience of the human spirit and the moments of clarity and calm that can emerge from the chaos.

In this book, you will find a series of poems that explore the depths of mental illness and the fight for mental wellness. The first section, **"Inner Battles,"** captures the intensity and often invisible nature of these struggles. The second section, **"Pursuit to Happiness,"** offers glimpses of hope and the various ways one can seek and find tranquility amidst the turmoil.

Whether you are personally affected by mental illness or seeking to understand it better, I hope these poems resonate with you. May they provide insight, comfort, and perhaps a new perspective on the complexities of mental health.

Thank you for joining me on this journey.

Acknowledgements

To everyone facing mental battles, especially the silent ones: this book is for you. Your strength and courage are what inspired these poems. I hope they offer you some comfort and remind you that you're not alone. Thank you for being a part of this journey and for your resilience.

Glossary

In this collection, I explore themes related to mental health and personal healing. Four poems reflect on the impact of psychological disorders, using terms that may not be familiar to everyone. To ensure clarity and a deeper connection to these experiences, I've included a glossary of key terms and abbreviations. These are not just words; they represent real internal struggles that many people face. I hope this helps foster greater understanding and empathy as you journey through these poems.

- **PTSD (Post-traumatic Stress Disorder)** [Page 6] – A disorder that develops in people that have experienced a shocking, scary, or dangerous event. Examples: Assault, natural disasters, death, abuse, accidents, etc.
- **DID (Dissociative Identity Disorder)** [Page 9] – A mental health condition where someone has two or more personalities that control their behavior at different times. It's sometimes also referred to as **Multiple Personality Disorder.**
- **PTED (Post-traumatic Embitterment Disorder)** [Page 11] – A pathological reaction to a negative life event, in which those experienced insult, humiliation, betrayal, and injustice. The emotions that one with PTED has includes: anger, hatred, and rage. They also fantasize about revenge.
- **OCD (Obsessive-Compulsive Disorder)** [Page 16] – A mental disorder where a person experiences uncontrollable, recurring thoughts, engages in repetitive behaviors, or both.

Table of Contents

Section 1: Inner Battles

Section 2: Pursuit to Happiness

Section 1: Inner Battles

Misophonia

The sounds of pens clicking,

People chewing and smacking,

Send me into a rage,

Like a lion,

Defending its den.

Each noise, an intrusion of my mind,

Invading my peace, fueling more anger.

A whirlwind of thoughts, no way to escape,

Trapped in chaos, feeling out of sync.

My hands, clenched and sweaty,

Muscles tensed and strained,

Seeking a release, trying to break this chain.

I close my eyes, count to ten,

Hoping for the calm to settle in.

The noise temporarily fades away,

A battle I face each and every day.

Anxiety Attack

I'm anxious, unable to find relief,

Desperate for healing to soothe my soul.

I'm shaking, feeling suffocated,

The frustration is overwhelming.

Breathing is hard, thoughts are spinning in circles,

My heart sinks to my stomach,

And it feels as if I've been on a quest.

This quest is never-ending.

And is making me face what's triggering me.

Each step reveals fears

I thought I'd overcome so long ago.

It feels as though my hard work was in vain,

Now I'm trapped in this endless race.

I long to feel and be normal, to escape from this chaotic reality,

And flee this emotional swarm.

Through the turmoil and endless quest,

A new vision of peace will take place.

The secret garden calls me,

A tranquil haven inviting me to finally rest, to find my way home.

Battle of Depression

I'm losing interest in everything,

And feel like I no longer belong here.

I feel like I'm trapped in a cold, dark ward,

With walls that close in and no windows to escape.

Always tired and achy, as if I've been run over.

Feeling numb and disconnected from the world,

My appetite decreasing, food tasteless.

My mind is a maze with no exit in sight,

Filled with unanswered questions and feelings.

Family and friends reach out, but their words

And pleas fade into the dark.

In this war, I've wandered far and wide,

The outcome remains obscured, a constant struggle.

It's my duty to make sure that I emerge from this battle with a victory.

Imposter Syndrome

Under the harsh glare of spotlights,

I step onto the stage, my heart drumming loud,

Yet, the loud whispers of my own self-doubt,

Force me to flee, questioning my own ability.

The crowd's cheers fade like distant memories,

Their faces pixelated, dissolving in the haze.

In the hallway, I grasp for breath,

Lost in silence, weighed down by regret.

Drowning in disappointment and shame,

The weight of failure bears against my chest.

Yet, as I sit in sorrow,

A glimmer of relief begins to shine.

A light breaks through the fuzziness,

Guiding me to clarity.

Slowly, I believe in myself,

My skills become clear, like truths revealed.

PTSD

I'm constantly on edge,

Haunted by flashbacks and nightmares.

They back me into a corner,

No escape, no exit—

Each moment replaying the past's relentless torment.

I've sought refuge in running away and numbing my pain,

Yet my scars deepen,

Both mental and physical.

I toss and turn in my sleep,

And sweat as though I've run a 4K race.

The past clings to me like an unbreakable headlock,

Choking me in its endless grasp.

Through the shadows, I've learned to navigate this dark path.

My scars are marks of survival.

This is my reality,

But it's up to me to find ways to manage and work through my PTSD.

Prolonged Grief Disorder

Life has been hard since you've been gone,

Especially since I never expected that our time together

Would be cut abruptly.

Since you've left,

I've felt a hole in my heart, an emptiness inside,

That nothing seems to fill.

My world is like a broken clock,

Stuck at the moment of your departure,

And unable to move forward.

Life and time have frozen in place,

Leaving me living in the past.

I feel as if the only way it will unfreeze

Is if you were still here.

I've stopped doing the things you've once loved,

Because they bring back memories that are hard to control.

I can't even watch your favorite shows without thinking of you,

Or even look at photographs and your items you left behind,

Without getting emotional.

Prolonged Grief Disorder

My appetite has majorly decreased,

My sleeping pattern is like a scratched record,

Where every night is a jarring interruption,

Never reaching the soothing lull of a full rest.

Sharp pains also hit me as if I've been stabbed.

I always find myself lost in thoughts of what could've been

Imagining a world where your smile and laughter still fills the room,

Where my days are not shadowed by your physical absence,

And our moments together are more than just distant memories.

This is the weight of prolonged grief,

Where you often live with memories,

Haunted by the "what ifs",

And the prolonged ache of a future that will never exist.

D.I.D

At four or five, beneath a veil of innocence,

A tornado swept through my young world, unseen.

To escape its fast fury, I scattered my soul,

Lost parts, feeding the tornado's furious swell.

In the storm's aftermath, winds of my mind,

Razed the land where memories were left behind.

Debris of the past scattered, lost in the whirlwind,

Amnesia's haze left my memories misaligned.

Within me, resides four distinct souls,

Each with a unique essence.

Quinn, a child of joy, in colors bright and bold,

Plays and explores with wonder, never growing old.

In a world of vibrant hues, they imagine and create with glee,

Their innocence, a beacon, letting their spirit run free.

Kai, a provider and protector in formal attire,

Takes charge with ease, never falling short,

In stressful moments, their strength and demeanor,

A rainbow so bright,

Guiding with purpose, like a halo of light.

Jordan, with a boho flair and creativity embraced,

Writes, photographs, and strums with grace.

A guitar's melody and a lens's focused eye,

Their art and passion entwined dreams that never die.

Kendall, a firecracker waiting to explode,

A temper that's headed down a volatile road.

Constantly seeing red at every spark,

Ready to flare up at the slightest remark.

Inside, a thunderstorm brews, shaky and loud,

Their rage, a roar in a dark cloud.

With every outburst, the storm's power unleashes,

Leaving chaos and tremors, shaking the world.

Though each soul within me has a unique story,

They blend together, forming a complex category.

In the journey of DID, they shape who I am,

Each soul persists, never letting me scram.

PTED

I can't escape the acrid taste of bitterness,

Lingering like plaque, tarnishing my tongue,

It clings to my palate,

A constant reminder of the wound,

An ember of anger, a boiling volcano,

Ready to erupt with unrestrained fury.

What happened to me was unfair and undeserved,

Which makes me feel as if my life has been cursed.

I feel like I'm in shackles and can't escape,

Bound by invisible chains of sorrow and regret.

My thoughts are consumed with visions of revenge,

Hoping my perpetrators face a hard reckoning.

The trust that I once had,

Has now faded in the wind,

Blown away like white smoke,

Disappearing without a trace.

My life will never be the same,

Consumed by ashes from a burning rage.

Haunted by Hallucinations

I hear loud and distinct voices.

They tell me that I'm a disappointment,

And that I will always be.

They scream, "You're a failure,"

"You should be ashamed of yourself,"

And, "Your behavior is awful, beyond repair."

Their voices back me into every confining space,

Like bullies lying in wait,

Ready to jerk me around,

And beat me down.

It makes me want to take out my brain.

All I can do is hold my head, run,

And scream, "Please leave me alone!"

It feels like ants are crawling on my skin,

And invisible eyes follow my every move.

I don't know where to go,

Or what to do.

Haunted by Hallucinations

I feel like a lost puppy in the woods,

With no clue where I am,

Or who to turn to for help.

Each moment seems like torture,

A war with my own mind.

Will this war ever end,

Or will I fight myself forever?

No More Settling

Dang, I really settled for less,

All while being distressed.

I let people make me feel as if I required too much,

Or that I was out of touch.

Out of touch with reality

And out of touch with my mentality.

I let them play me like a fiddle,

Only feeding me crumbs.

I felt like an abandoned building, lost and left astray.

All from letting my mental health slip like a thief in the night,

I was left to mend it all myself, like a solitary craftsman.

The excruciating pain, both mental and physical,

Having settled for so long, haunts me daily.

A cruel reminder of how I was treated unfairly.

The thought of it makes me sick to my stomach,

And makes me want to hurl.

It makes me also want to hide under a rock, consumed by shame.

No More Settling

I've learned my lesson the hard way.

No more settling, no more being swayed,

I'm upgrading my life, stepping up to a new grade.

OCD

In a room where the door never opens,

Thoughts crowd like uninvited guests.

Words of contamination loudly linger —

Every surface a battleground, every touch a risk.

Hands perform in a rhythmic dance beneath the faucet's warm gaze,

Each scrub with antibacterial soap, a choreography that never ends.

The weight of endless washing sinks deep,

Leaving me with no peace.

In the silence of each ritual's darkness,

The hands ache and the heart grows fatigued,

Yet, the cycle turns on relentless—

A delicate attempt to hold back the battle.

As the rhythm of cleansing fades,

The scan shifts to the door and corners,

Each turn of the lock, a gentle comfort,

Each object repositioned, an intermittent touch of reassurance.

With the last objects finally checked,

The stillness feels like a daydream—

Is this calmness a scheme?

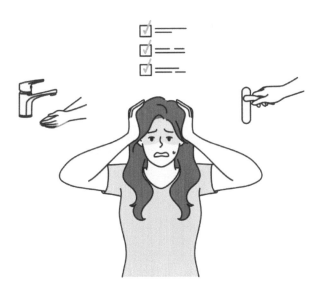

Addiction's Mirror

This daily addiction to drugs, alcohol, and pills,

Is all becoming too much,

To where I can't continue to cope like this.

I feel like my world is crashing down,

And as if I'm moving in slow motion.

The aftereffects make me feel nauseous,

And as if I'm a zombie.

I've pushed my friends and family away,

All to get rid of this temporary pain.

I've lashed out and caused havoc,

And now I'm faced with the aftermath,

It's tragic.

As I look in the mirror, I see a stranger,

With a dark soul that's in danger.

I've lost my way,

And I know that I can't keep living this way.

It's time to break free from this loop,

And regroup, rebuild what's been torn.

It's only right because I've caused so much harm.

Narcissistic Ride

Dating me is a thrilling headache,

A constant whirlwind of confusion and fascination.

I present myself as a rare, shiny prize,

In a world of the mundane.

My aura is irresistible, a colorful mask that conceals,

Covering the cracks that distort the reality beneath.

I shape the truths like a puppet master,

Orchestrating them with precisions.

You begin to doubt your own reflection and reality,

Until both become distortions in my grand narrative.

Lost in the tangle of deceptions and mind games,

You navigate through my storm of doubts and manipulation.

Every step feels like walking on eggshells,

Every path filled with uncertainty.

Narcissistic Ride

As you strive to escape my mental grip I've skillfully designed,

You struggle to break free from my matrix of control.

Evading my empty promises,

And untangling my illusions,

You fight to rediscover your true identity.

In your ultimate escape from my imaginative world,

You breathe the soothing air of independence and freedom,

Finally free from the cage I built.

Body Dysmorphia

I'm trapped in a playground with my own reflection,
A relentless struggle that breeds deep rejection.

My heart and mind are all filled with sadness,
And a flood of tears.
This sadness feels like I'm grieving a lost loved one.
But the loss is of myself,
The person I was or wish I could become.

I never want to leave my house,
Because I can't function well.
If I could stay here forever, I'd hide from judgement
I project onto every gaze.

When I'm in public, I wish I was invisible,
So no one can see me,
So no can see the cracks I'm convinced they notice.

In my mind, I'm shaped like a whale,
A vast expanse of imperfection.

Body Dysmorphia

My face, a cratered landscape,

Etched with flaws that I can't escape.

Caught in this endless of self-loathing,

Where every flaw magnified feels like a burden,

Too heavy to carry.

Hoping for the day where my reflection feels like home,

Where I can finally love the person I've always criticized.

Section 2: Pursuit to Happiness

Heal Your Inner Child

Do you remember the moments
In your childhood that made you happy?

Like riding your bike down dirt or gravel roads,
The wind, a gentle whisper, carefree on those roads?

Or surfing the web on your throwback desktop,
Getting lost in online games, message boards, or music videos?

Maybe even creating choreography with your cousins,
While giggles and rhythms fill the room
Or waking up on Saturday mornings to catch
shows on Nickelodeon, KIDS' WB, or Disney?

These key fragments of your past,
Are steadfast bridges to healing.
Return to these simple, carefree days,
And let their magic guide your way.

Revisit the happiness that once seemed blue,
And let the memories live through you.

Heal Your Inner Child

Let the cherished moments be your means,

And let your inner child and joy, sing.

Journey of Forgiveness

What does it mean to find peace

In the midst of a tornado?

Forgiving doesn't erase their wrongs.

You simply dispose the burdens that were never yours to carry.

Forgiveness is a gift to yourself,

For your peace and sanity,

It's about freeing your soul and spirit from the fire they ignited.

In letting go, you find the calmness in the ocean,

Where once there were turbulent waves,

The loud noises of conflict and anger fade away,

Leading you to brighter days.

Sometimes, the hardest part is looking in the mirror,

And looking within to forgive yourself,

For self-forgiveness is the first step towards true healing,

Clearing the pathway for tranquility and renewal.

In forgiving, you unlock the door,

Opening the way to embrace others with grace,

Journey of Forgiveness

For it is peace that turns the key,

Revealing the hidden path to true forgiveness.

Gratitude

Life is what you make of it.

Even when it feels like life is bringing you a flood,

Seek out the treasures in the storm,

The pieces that are valuable and remind you of what you're grateful for.

Through the storm's debris, we grow stronger,

Clinging to hope as we drift along longer.

Life's blessings often lie in simple things,

The joyous moments shared with loved ones,

The warmth of a home, a cozy hug from a friend —

These are simple gifts where gratitude begins.

Embrace the love and laughter around the room,

For every day doesn't have to be filled with gloom.

Gratitude is about finding the simple joys and moments,

The ones that cling to you like a comforting home.

In these moments, we all have something to be grateful for.

Gratitude drifts to us, gently floating ashore.

Letting Go of Guilt

The trauma that happened to you,

Is not your fault.

The mental disorders or illnesses you have,

Don't make you less than.

You are a unique individual with superpowers,

Remind yourself of that every hour.

The guilt you're harboring, is not yours to carry.

Embrace your strength and let yourself be merry.

You deserve a life of freedom,

And to feel as if you live in a kingdom.

As you walk through this journey, remember this truth:

You're enough, worthy, and full of proof.

So, love on and hug yourself tight,

With all your might, through every day and night.

Affirmations

Affirmations are wings that help me rise,
Above the doubt in fears, into clearer skies.

With every affirmation, my wings unfold,
Lifting me to dreams that are to be told.
In the sky, I boldly soar,
Embracing the paths I dream to explore.

I've finally found the peace and happiness I've longed for,
With every smile and breath, I inhale the calm and more.

It took a while to get to this journey,
But now I embrace every moment,
Free and always learning.

Thank you, God, my guides, and affirmations,
For leading me in the right direction.
I won't disappoint you all, moving forward with no hesitation.

I'm eternally grateful for the guidance that struts my way,
I move forward with hope in my heart, each day.

Finding Beauty

♥ ♥ ♥

Do you know what makes you beautiful?

Your flaws,

Your honesty,

Your personality,

Your scars,

Your way of thinking.

And even when the dark fog clouds your mind,

You're still beautiful,

In the courage it takes to rise each day,

In the way you fight,

In the gentleness of your heart,

You are more than the battles you conquer.

When the mirror displays a different view,

Seek the things you love within yourself.

The traits that make you smile,

Bringing comfort to your heart,

The passions that make your soul tingle.

Finding Beauty

♥ ♥ ♥

Let these views remind you,

That beauty is not just seen, but felt—

It's about finding the light within your soul and heart.

Let Your Hair Down

Let your hair down,

And quit being so uptight.

Loosen up your tight grip,

And let the moments ignite.

Untense your muscles, let go of the strain,

You no longer deserve to worry or be in pain.

Keep in mind, we are all different,

And heading down our own windy paths.

So embrace your unique aspects,

And let go of all the possible aftermaths.

Imagine the layers that shed as you drop your defenses,

Feeling the gentle, cold breeze,

As your guard fades and you let your hair down,

You will be at so much ease.

Take baby steps towards the openness you're seeking,

Trust the genuine voice that's speaking.

Allow yourself to trust, grow, and let go,

Embrace the treasures your heart and soul are revealing.

Savor each moment and let your soul glow.

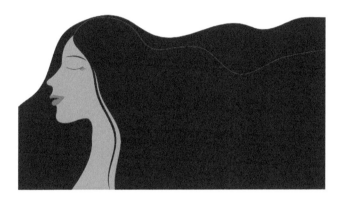

Healthy Outlets

When anger arises, hot and conflagrate[1],
A fire within, too fierce to abate,
Don't let it consume you, or get out of control,
Find a safe way to release and console.

Put on the gloves, strike with all your might,
Box out the rage and reclaim your sight.
Or pick up a pen or pencil, let your thoughts flow,
Write it down, let the emotions show.

Sing it out, let your voice be free,
Or scream as loud as you can, and let it be.
Play a singing bowl, let the vibrations range,
Let the soothing tones help you rearrange.

Pick up a brush, explore colors freely,
Paint your anger, let it flow completely.
When the storm inside starts to boil,
Throw something safely, let the tension uncoil.

Conflagrate – To start burning or burst into flames.[1]

Explore each path, stick with what feels right,

To release your anger healthily, and brighten your light

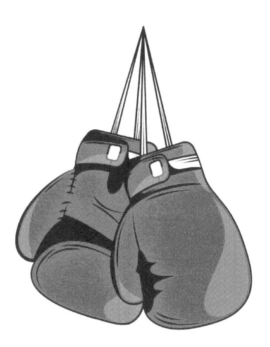

A Toast to You

Raise your glass high to the challenges you've won,

And your goals that lie ahead.

This is your time to shine,

After hanging by a thread.

Toast to the courage,

That brought you through your darkest days,

And the moments that ignited you,

Lighting up your ways.

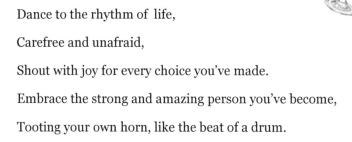

Dance to the rhythm of life,

Carefree and unafraid,

Shout with joy for every choice you've made.

Embrace the strong and amazing person you've become,

Tooting your own horn, like the beat of a drum.

Celebrate as if there's no tomorrow,

And allow yourself to no longer live in sorrow.

You've done the work to get to this point in life,

And you deserve to be happy and thrive.

Puzzle of Transition

We've all made choices that we regret,

And those choices, we struggle to forget.

We dwell on these decisions,

Trapped in a cycle of our past's revisions.

They hold us in a tight embrace,

Leaving us with abundant disgrace.

Though the past has left its impactful mark,

We must move forward, igniting a spark.

Our choices, though they linger and sway,

Are lessons that guide us on our way.

It's never too late to seek what you need,

To address the struggles and plant new seeds,

With guidance and hope we solve the puzzle,

Finding strength as we navigate the hustle.

Boundary Lines

Learn to build a wall, sturdy and kind,

To shield your heart and guard your mind.

A palace of peace, where love can thrive,

Protecting the essence that lives inside.

Through the chaos, draw the lines,

For your mental health and peaceful times.

Build a wall of tranquility, not to isolate,

But to keep the turmoil and distractions away.

Seek support, extend your hand,

Boundaries help you take a stand.

Protect your spirit, guard your heart,

In this safe space, play it smart.

Self-Care Symphony

Take care of your body, let it rest and grow,

Fuel it with positive things, let your energy flow.

Move every day, even if it's just a little bit,

Release the tension with a stretch, don't let yourself sit.

Take care of your mind, give it a break,

Cut out the noise with a book or music, for your own sake.

Rest when you're fatigued, don't push through the aches,

Allow yourself to take short or long breaks,

Like a restful slumber or a peaceful escape.

Take care of your soul, feed it with your joy,

Find what you love, let your heart enjoy.

Cherish each moment, let your spirit play,

Groove through your days with a dance, let your heart sway.

Connect with Me!

Thank you for reading *Mental Warfare*! I'd love to hear from you and keep you updated on my latest work.

Connect with me and stay in touch:

- **Social Media**:

    - Facebook: Breuna Walker or www.facebook.com/SincerelyBreuna/

    - X/Twitter: @SincerelyBreuna

    - Instagram: @_QueenBreuna and @BresPositiveSpace

    - TikTok: @SincerelyBreuna

Check out my debut book**:** *"Heartstrings and Reflections"*– Available now on Amazon.

Exciting news: *Mental Warfare* is just the beginning. Part 2 will be out sometime next year! Stay tuned for more.

I'd also greatly appreciate your feedback! If you enjoyed this book, please consider leaving a review on Amazon or Goodreads. Your reviews help other readers find my work and make a big difference.